THINGS IN THE CLASSROOM

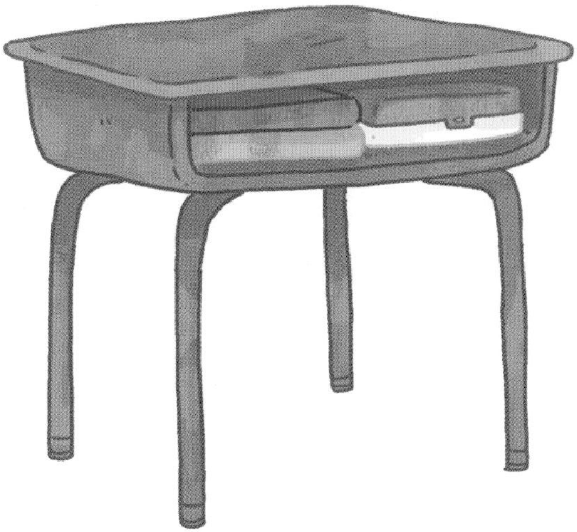

ILLUSTRATED BY

Ali Hinch

board

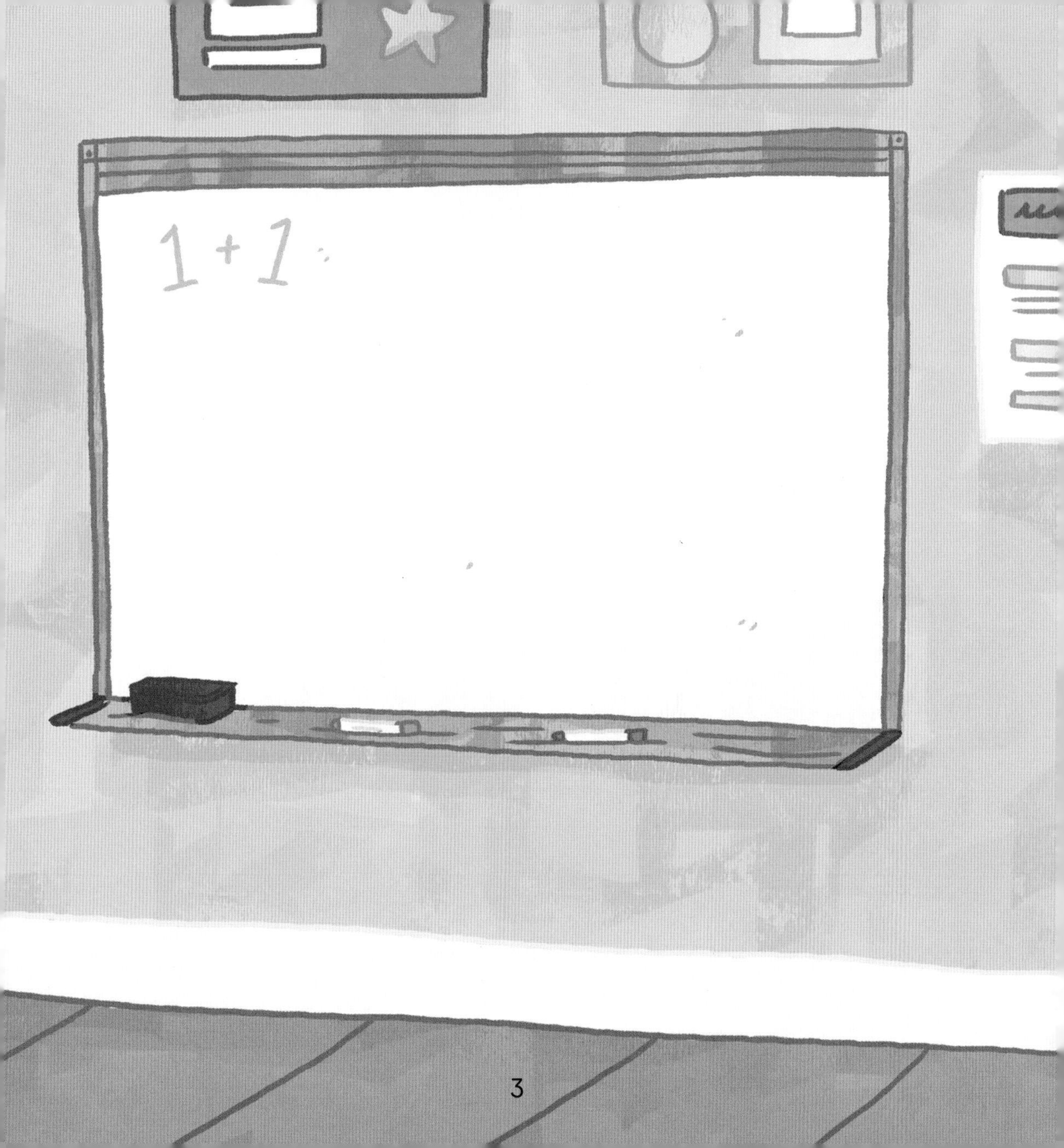
1+1

book

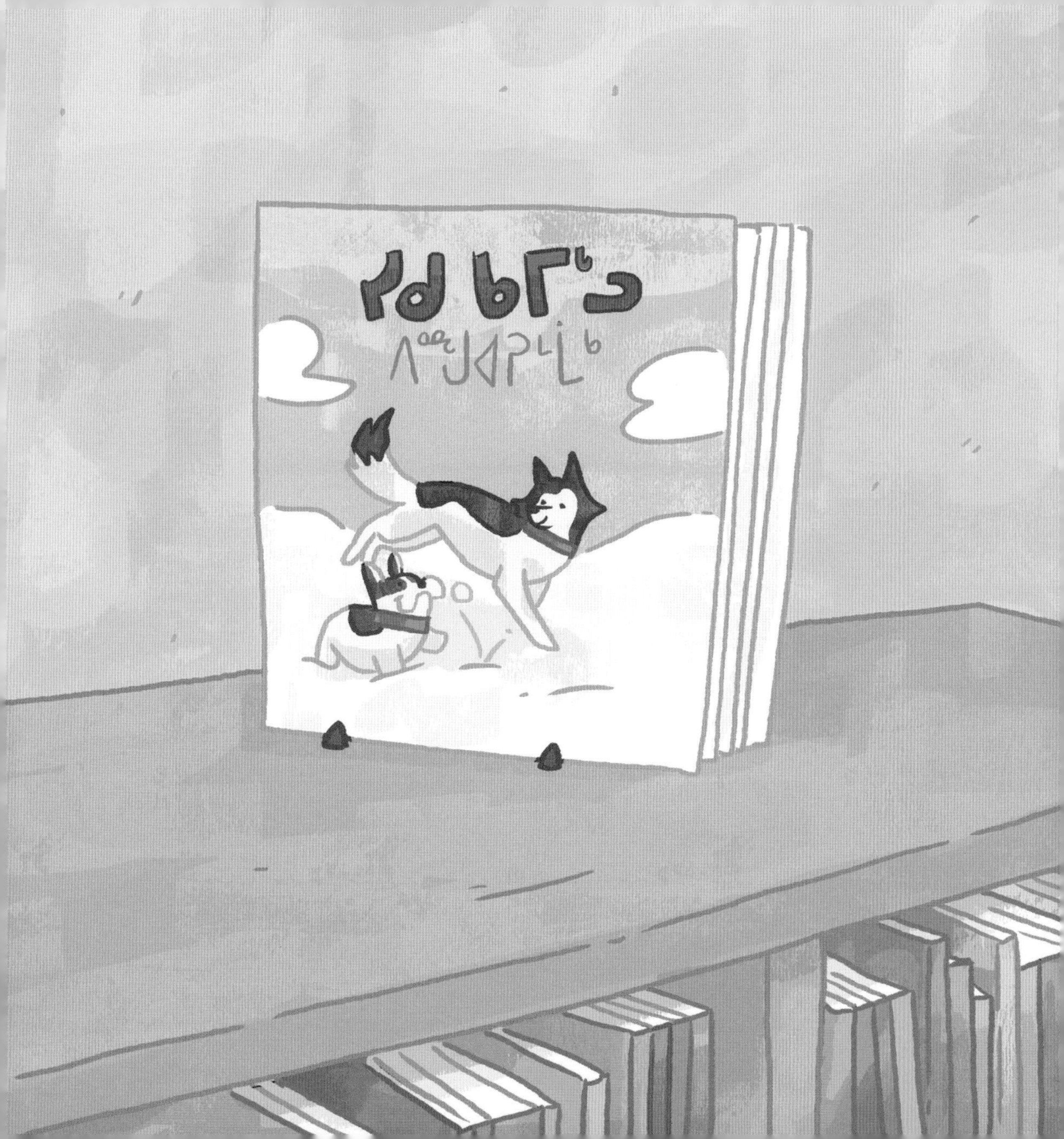
ᓯᑯ ᑲᒥᒃᑐ

clock

12
1
2
3
4
5
6
7
8
9
10
11

desk

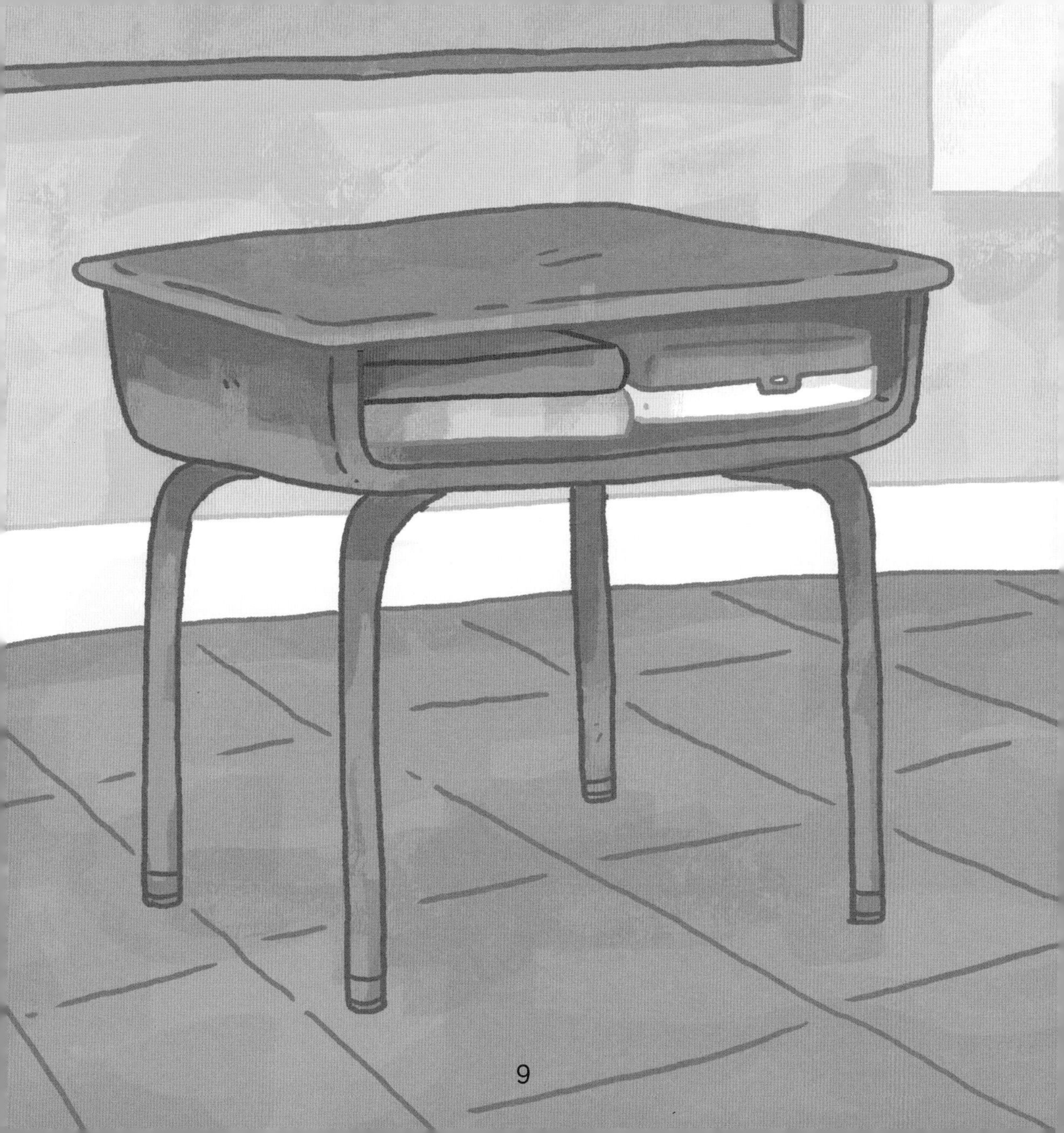

table

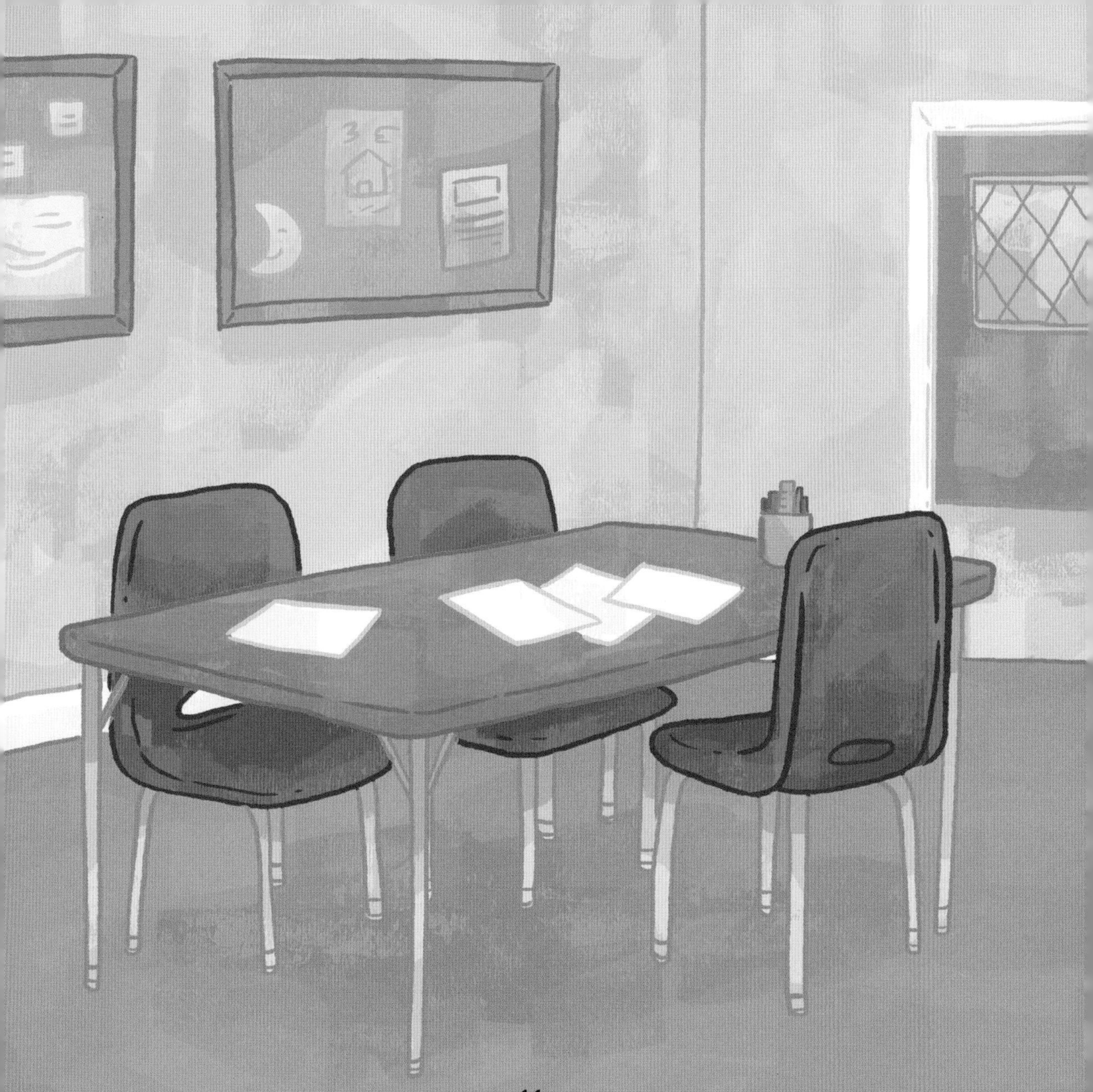

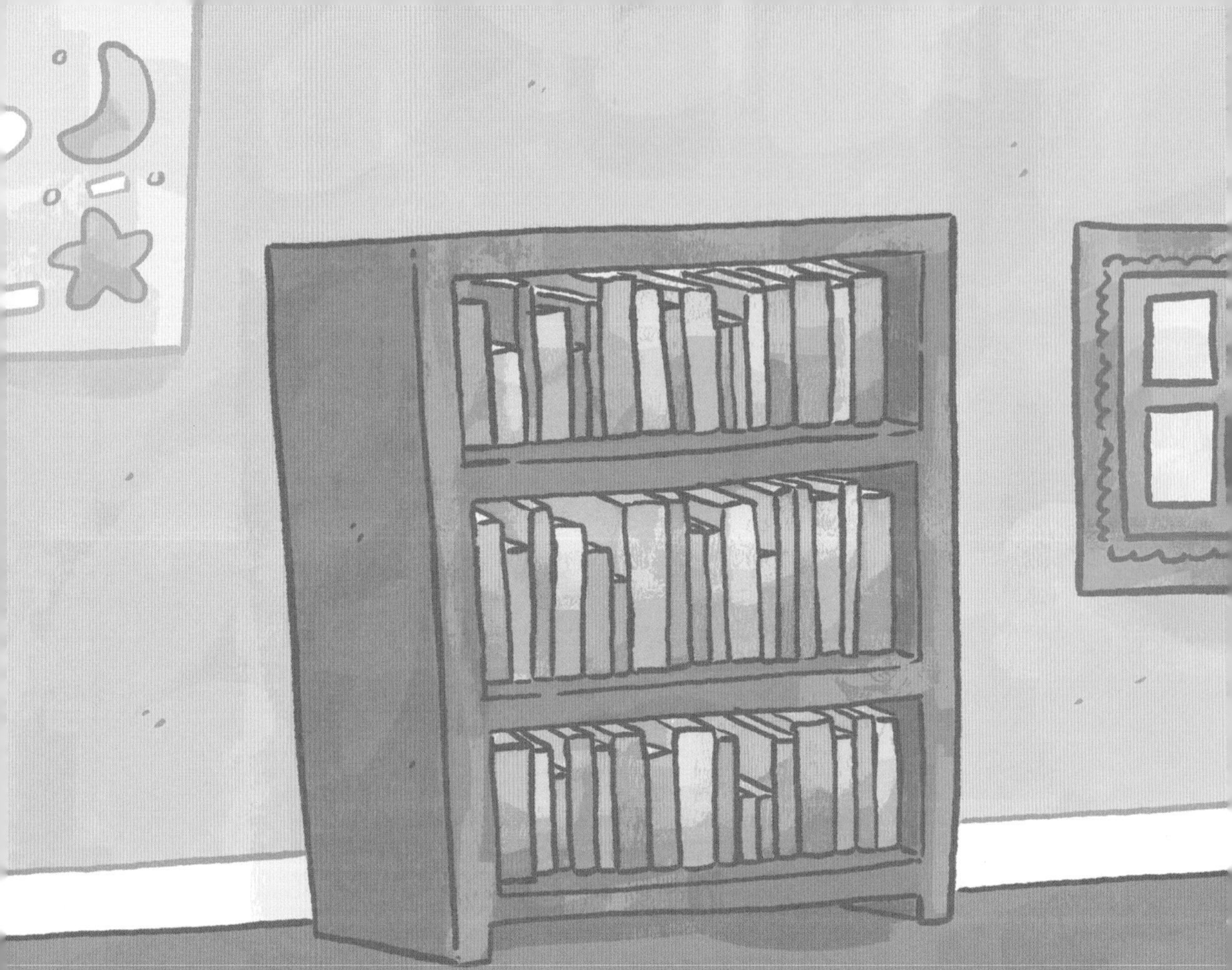

bookcase